SYNCOPATION ETUDES
FOR
SNARE DRUM

BY JOEL ROTHMAN

ISBN 978-1-5400-2303-2

Visit Hal Leonard Online at
www.halleonard.com

Contact Us:
Hal Leonard
7777 West Bluemound Road
Milwaukee, WI 53213
Email: info@halleonard.com

In Europe contact:
Hal Leonard Europe Limited
42 Wigmore Street
Marylebone, London, W1U 2RN
Email: info@halleonardeurope.com

In Australia contact:
Hal Leonard Australia Pty. Ltd.
4 Lentara Court
Cheltenham, Victoria, 3192 Australia
Email: info@halleonard.com.au

DEDICATION

I dedicate this book to my children, grandchildren, and to my beautiful, loving, and devoted wife.

I would also like to thank all the people who have helped me in the production of my books throughout the years, as well as the multitude of drum and percussion teachers worldwide who have seen fit to use them with their students.

CONTENTS

INTRODUCTION

As the title implies, this study presents an extensive array of etudes focusing especially on syncopated rhythmic patterns in quarter time as well as eighth time. It is presumed the reader understands the breakdown of rhythm, and is capable of reading quarter notes, eighth notes, 16th notes, triplets, and dotted rhythms.

Although dynamics are included, they are sparsely sprinkled throughout each etude so the eye is focused firmly on reading the patterns of syncopated rhythms with as little distraction as possible. Initially, I suggest you omit the dynamics and first concentrate on developing accuracy and speed with the rhythmic makeup in each etude. At that point, play the etude again and include the dynamics. If you would like to make the reading more challenging, pencil in extra dynamics wherever you feel it's appropriate. A single grace note is attached to certain notes to form flams, but you can add extra grace notes to create drags or the single-stroke four whenever you think it's warranted.

Tempo indications are omitted. Simply develop each etude to the best of your ability. Practicing with a metronome will help to ensure an accurate and consistent pulse.

Syncopation Etudes can be thought of as a follow-up to Ted Reed's excellent book, *Syncopation for the Modern Drummer*. This study, however, delves deeper into the subject within the highly musical format of etudes at an intermediate level.

Aside from executing the etudes on the snare exactly as written, there are dozens of different ways they can be played to further develop various skills, and the following suggestions are just a few of the possibilities:

1. Play each of the etudes on the snare with single strokes leading with your favored hand, then play it again and reverse the sticking.

2. In etudes with just quarter notes and eighth notes, try swinging the eighth notes with a jazz-triplet feel.

3. Replay selected etudes by keeping a steady eighth-note rock cymbal beat with one hand, then play the notes of the etude with the other hand on the snare, or between the snare and tom-toms.

4. Replay selected etudes by playing a steady jazz cymbal beat with one hand, then swing the eighth notes in the etude with a jazz-triplet feel with the other hand on the snare and tom-toms.

5. Instead of playing the etude only on a snare, divide the notes between the snare drum and bass drum.

6. Play the entire etude with your feet instead of your hands.

The list goes on and on, so create your own ways of utilizing the different etudes after each is mastered as written.

PART ONE

Syncopation Etudes with Quarter and Eighth Notes in 3/4, 4/4, and 5/4 Time

Simply put, to the listening ear, syncopation is the sound of stressed or accented offbeats. When it comes to reading rhythmic notation, however, the sound of syncopation is produced when quarter notes and dotted-quarter notes, which normally fall on a downbeat, instead fall on the upbeat.

When notated, there are six basic syncopated patterns with quarter notes and dotted-quarter notes in quarter time, not including patterns with ties:

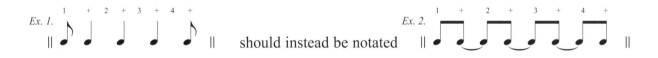

Extended to 4/4 time, you might see these patterns including ties:

While, theoretically correct, it could rightly be argued that notating consecutive quarter notes on the upbeat, as seen in the following Example 1, is incorrect writing because in 4/4 time each half of the bar should be seen clearly, and consecutive quarter notes on the upbeat obscures both halves.

The rhythm sounds the same in both examples, but in Example 2 you can clearly see each half of the bar, whereas that's not true in Example 1.

A contradictory argument might be that consecutive quarter notes on the upbeat allow for fewer notes to be written to produce the same rhythm. Consequently, drummers must view and translate only five notes instead of eight notes with three ties, enabling them to read faster. Moreover, the arranger can save time by scripting fewer notes. Regardless of whether or not the notation is theoretically correct, it is commonly seen on arrangements, and some of the following etudes contain a rhythmic makeup with consecutive quarter notes on the upbeat. (See especially Etudes 17-22.)

ETUDE 1
FEATURING

ETUDE 2

For added practice, try interpreting the eighth notes with a jazz-triplet feel:

ETUDE 3

ETUDE 4

ETUDE 5
FEATURING

ETUDE 6

ETUDE 7

ETUDE 8

ETUDE 9
FEATURING

ETUDE 10

ETUDE 11

ETUDE 12

ETUDE 13
FEATURING

ETUDE 14

ETUDE 15

ETUDE 16

ETUDE 17

FEATURING

ETUDE 18

FEATURING

ETUDE 19

ETUDE 20

ETUDE 21
FEATURING

ETUDE 22
FEATURING

MIXING METERS
ETUDE 23

ETUDE 24

The following four etudes are comprised only of eighth notes with varied accents, producing a very syncopated sound. Play the etudes with single strokes, first with your lead hand, then reverse the sticking. You can also swing the eighth notes by playing them with a jazz-triplet feel, as mentioned in a previous footnote. For added practice, play the notes around the drums, placing all accented notes on a tom tom and unaccented notes on the snare.

ETUDE 25

ETUDE 26

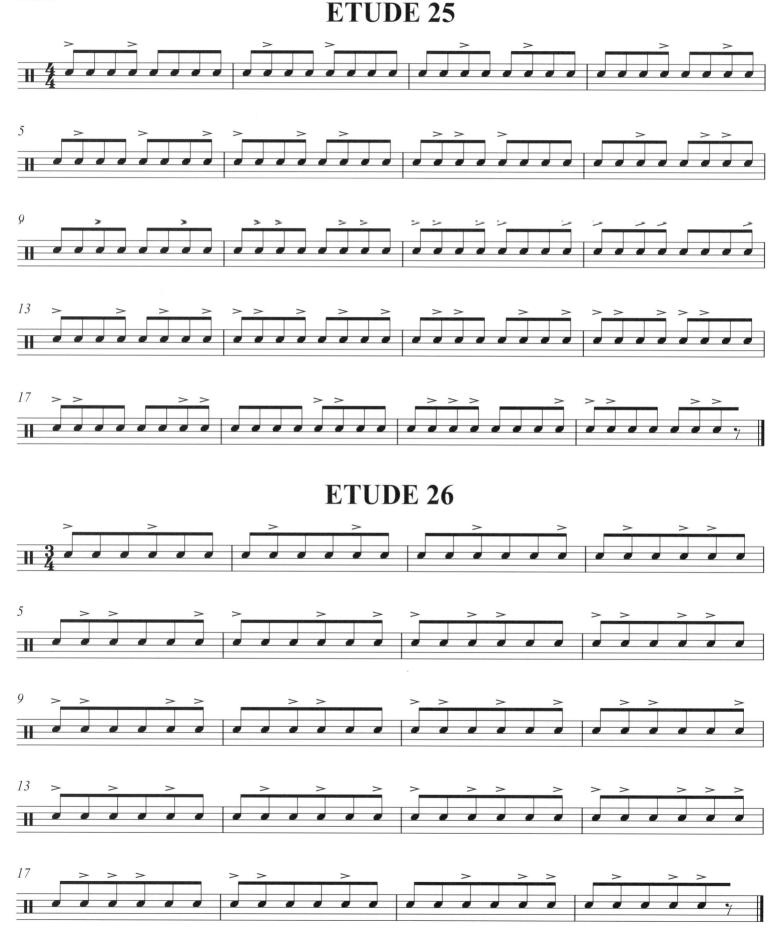

ETUDE 27

ETUDE 28

PART TWO

Syncopation Etudes with Quarter Notes, Eighth Notes, and Eighth-Note Triplets in 3/4, 4/4, and 5/4 Time

The etudes in this section are similar to the preceding etudes, but they now include eighth-note triplets. Remember, for added practice try interpreting the regular eighth notes with a jazz-triplet feel:

ETUDE 29

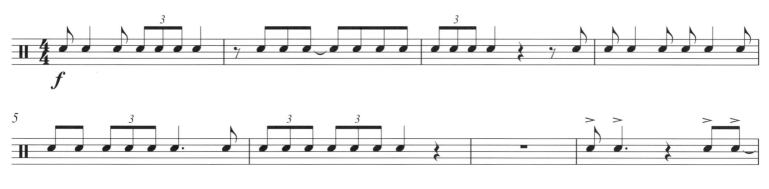

ETUDE 30

ETUDE 31

ETUDE 32

ETUDE 33

ETUDE 34

MIXING METERS
ETUDE 35

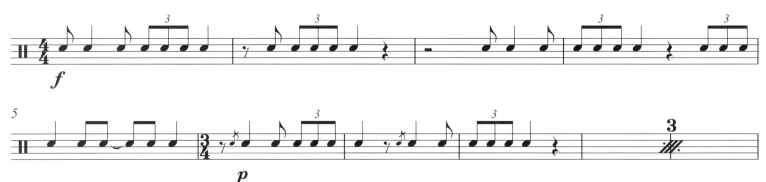

ETUDE 36

PART THREE

Syncopation Etudes with Syncopated Eighth-Note Triplets in Quarter Time

When notated, there are nine syncopated eighth-note triplet patterns, not including patterns with ties.

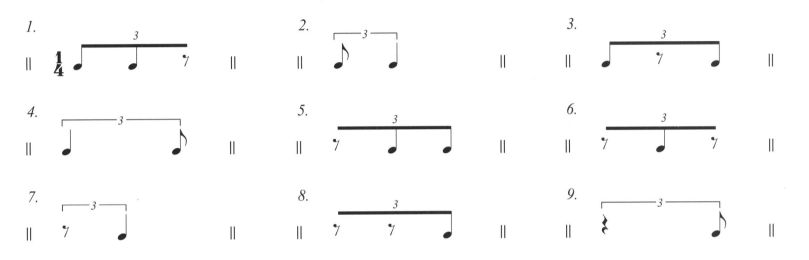

NOTE: The term "syncopated triplets" as I use it simply refers to the playing of parts of a triplet rather than the complete three notes.

ETUDE 37
FEATURING

ETUDE 39
FEATURING

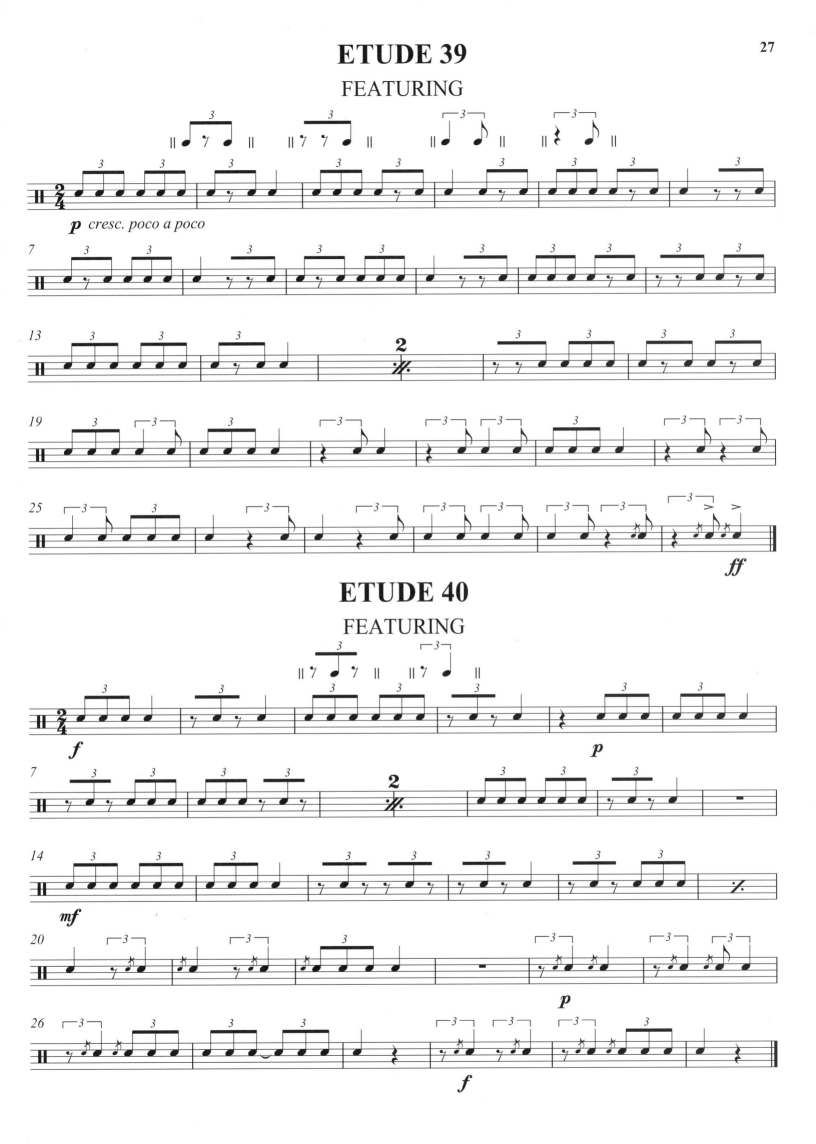

ETUDE 41
SUMMARY

ETUDE 42
SUMMARY

ETUDE 43
SUMMARY

ETUDE 44
SUMMARY

The following two etudes are set in compound meter, with three eighth notes comprising each beat. Accents occur on different parts of the beat, producing a very syncopated sound. Play the etudes with single strokes, first with your lead hand, then reverse the sticking. And once again, try playing the notes around the drums, placing all accented notes on a tom-tom and unaccented notes on the snare.

ETUDE 45

ETUDE 46

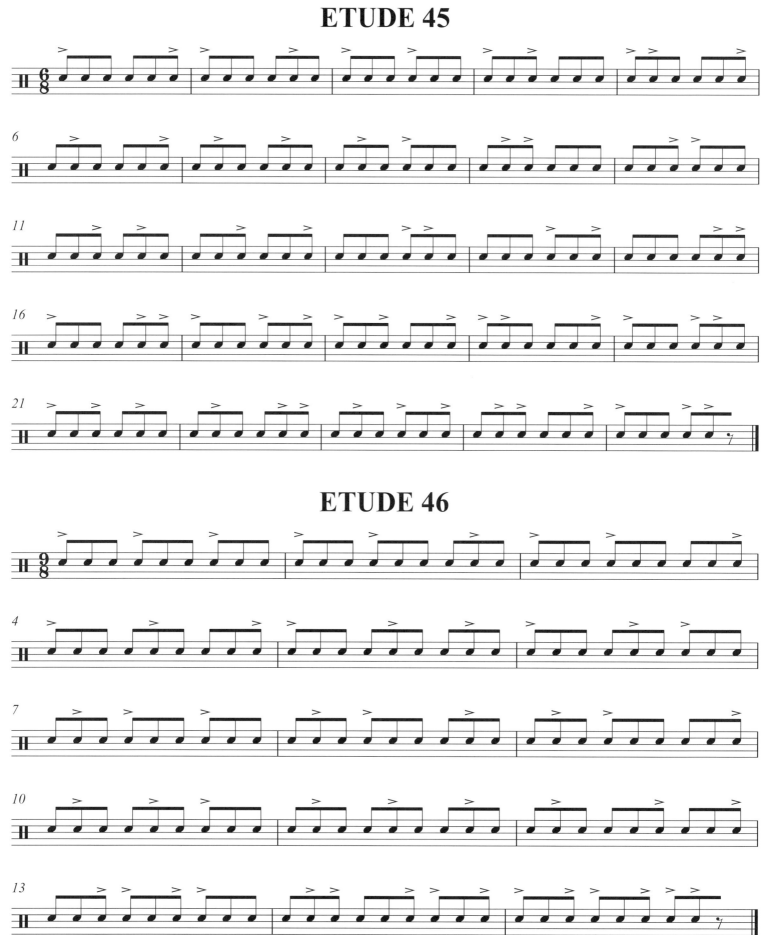

PART FOUR

Syncopation Etudes with Quarter, Eighth, and 16th Notes

In this section you will be presented with etudes containing the basic quarter-note and eighth-note syncopated rhythms, but the eighth notes will sometimes be subdivided into 16th notes.

Basic Syncopated Pattern:

Subdivided as follows:

ETUDE 47
FEATURING

ETUDE 49

FEATURING

ETUDE 50

ETUDE 51
FEATURING

ETUDE 52

ETUDE 53

FEATURING

ETUDE 54

PART FIVE

Syncopation Etudes with Eighth and 16th Notes, Including 16th Triplets

When it comes to eighth notes and 16th notes, the sound of syncopation is produced when eighth notes, which normally fall on a downbeat or upbeat, instead fall on the second part of a group of four 16th notes – on the count of "e." It also occurs when dotted-eighth notes, which normally fall only on a downbeat, also fall instead on the second part of a group of four 16th notes.

There are six basic syncopated rhythmic patterns with eighth notes, dotted-eighth notes, and 16th notes, not including patterns with ties:

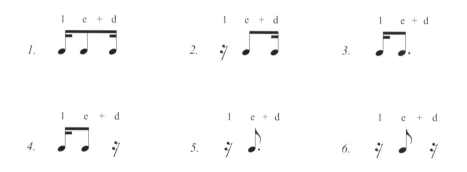

ETUDE 55

FEATURING

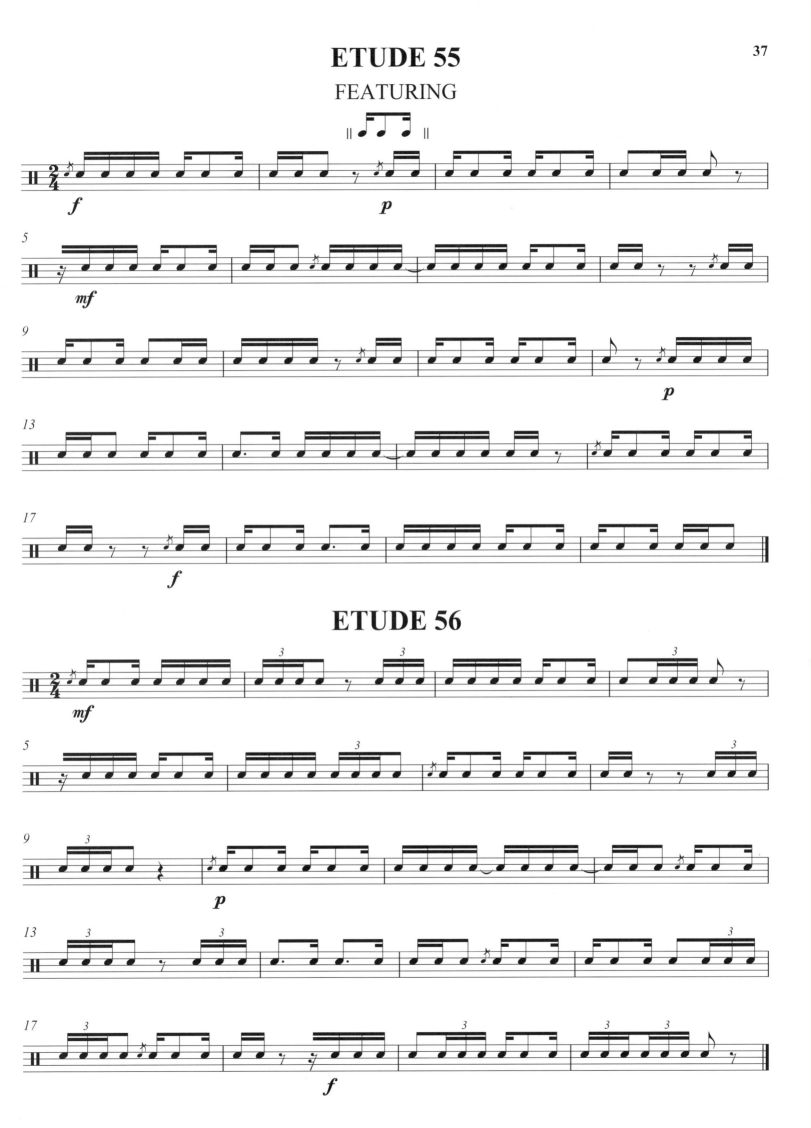

ETUDE 57
FEATURING

ETUDE 58

ETUDE 59
FEATURING

ETUDE 61
FEATURING

ETUDE 62

In the following two etudes, accented 16th notes produce a syncopated sound.

ETUDE 63

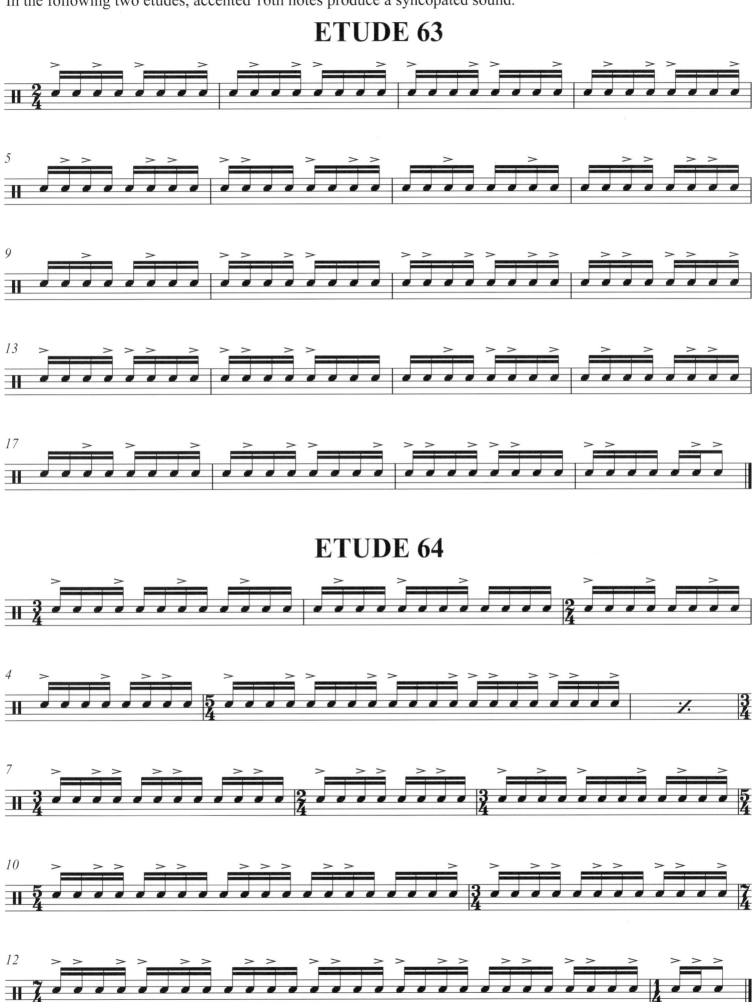

ETUDE 64

PART SIX

Syncopation Etudes with Eighth and 16th Notes, Including 16th Triplets in Eighth Time

ETUDE 65

FEATURING

ETUDE 67
FEATURING

ETUDE 68

ETUDE 69
FEATURING

ETUDE 71
FEATURING

ETUDE 72

ETUDE 73
SUMMARY

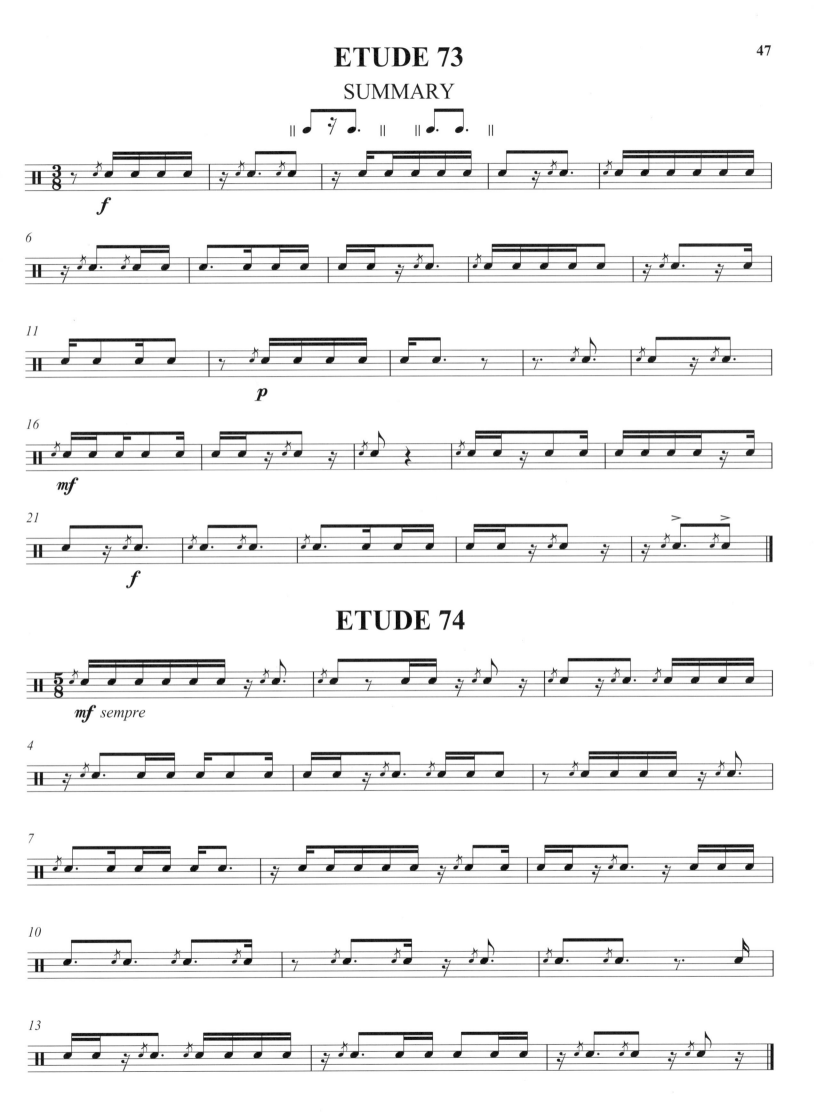

ETUDE 75
SUMMARY

ETUDE 76
SUMMARY

PART SEVEN

Syncopation Etudes with Rolls
in Quarter and Eighth Time

Practice with both open and closed rolls.

ETUDE 77

FEATURING

ETUDE 78

ETUDE 79
FEATURING

ETUDE 80

ETUDE 81
FEATURING

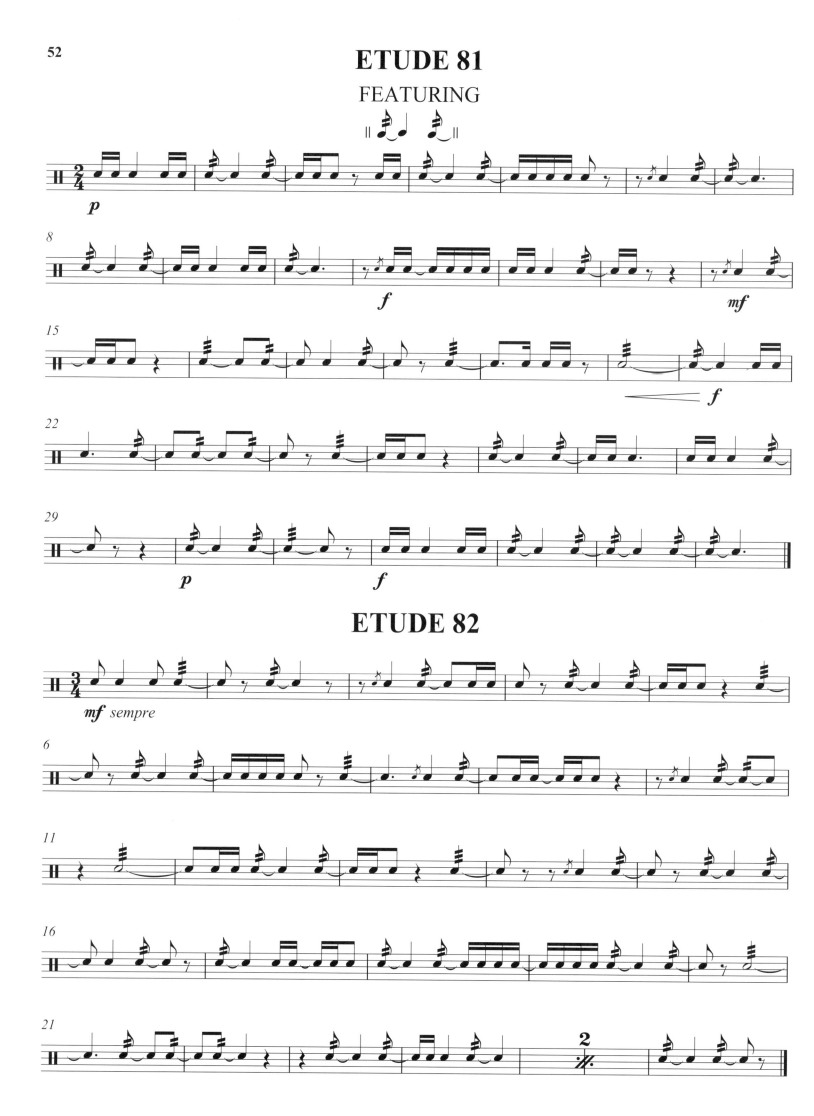

ETUDE 83

FEATURING

ETUDE 84

ETUDE 85

FEATURING

ETUDE 86

ETUDE 87

ETUDE 88

ETUDE 89

ETUDE 90